Get Off, Bug!

Written by Isabel Thomas
Illustrated by Sian Roberts

RISING STARS

Bill kicks a log.

A big fat bug is in the muck.

Bill pops the bug into a tin.

Bill pops the tin on the bed.

Nick huffs and puffs.

The bug is not in the tin!

Bill has a big bad fuss.

The bug is on his cuff.

Nick
Bad luck, Bill!

Get off, bug!

Talk about the story

Ask your child these questions:

1 Where did Bill find the big bug?

2 Who had a book about bugs?

3 How did the bug get out of the tin?

4 Why do you think Nick was pleased to see the bug?

5 Have you ever found a big bug? What did it look like?

6 What would you do if a big bug landed on you?

Can your child retell the story in their own words?